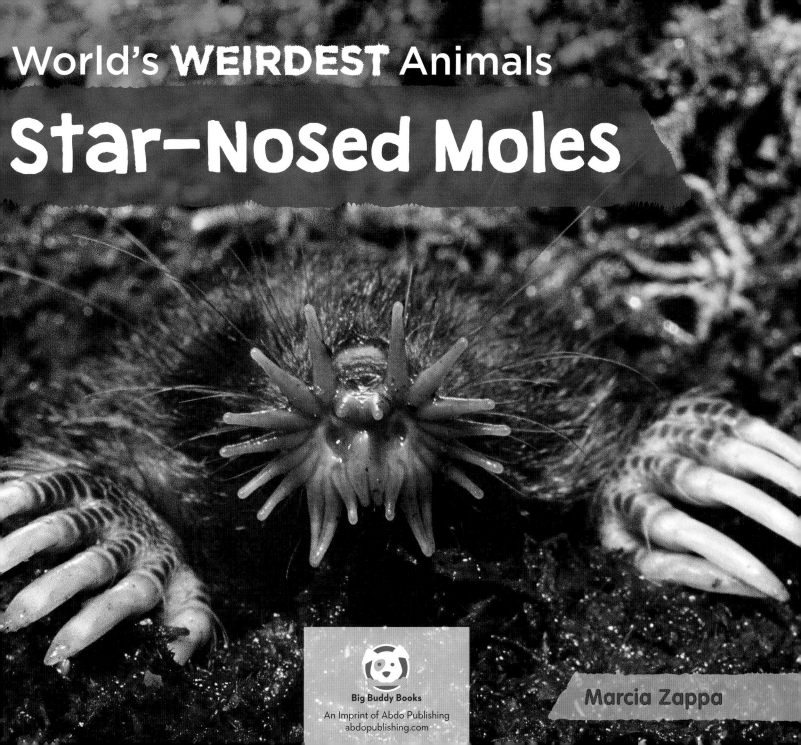

World's **WEIRDEST** Animals

Star-Nosed Moles

Big Buddy Books
An Imprint of Abdo Publishing
abdopublishing.com

Marcia Zappa

abdopublishing.com

Published by Abdo Publishing, a division of ABDO, PO Box 398166, Minneapolis, Minnesota 55439. Copyright © 2016 by Abdo Consulting Group, Inc. International copyrights reserved in all countries. No part of this book may be reproduced in any form without written permission from the publisher. Big Buddy Books™ is a trademark and logo of Abdo Publishing.

Printed in the United States of America, North Mankato, Minnesota.
042015
092015

Cover Photos: Visuals Unlimited, Inc./Ken Catania/Getty Images; Shutterstock.com.
Interior Photos: Ann Brokelman Photography (p. 21); Lynwood Chace/FLPA/Minden Pictures (p. 5); ER Degginger/Science Source (pp. 7, 9, 15); Degginger, Phil/Animals Animals - Earth Scenes (p. 23); Dembinsky Photo Ass./FLPA/Minden Pictures (p. 29); Habicht, Michael/Animals Animals - Earth Scenes (p. 19); Hillbraith/flickr.com (p. 27); Leszczynski, Zigmund/Animals Animals - Earth Scenes (p. 11); S & D & K Maslowski/FLPA/Minden Pictures (p. 17); Todd Pusser/NPL/Minden Pictures (p. 30); Specker, Donald/Animals Animals - Earth Scenes (p. 25).

Coordinating Series Editor: Rochelle Baltzer
Contributing Editors: Megan M. Gunderson, Bridget O'Brien, Sarah Tieck
Graphic Design: Adam Craven

Library of Congress Cataloging-in-Publication Data

Zappa, Marcia, 1985- author.
  Star-nosed moles / Marcia Zappa.
     pages cm. -- (World's weirdest animals)
  ISBN 978-1-62403-778-8
1. Star-nosed mole--Juvenile literature. I. Title.
  QL737.S76Z37 2016
  599.33'5--dc23
                    2015005571

Contents

Wildly Weird!

The world is full of weird, wonderful animals. Star-nosed moles are small **mammals**. They live in North America.

This unusual animal has **tentacles** surrounding its nose! These super-**sensitive** feelers help the mole move underground and find food. This feature makes star-nosed moles wildly weird!

No other mammal in the world has a nose like the star-nosed mole.

Bold Bodies

A star-nosed mole's body is covered in thick, short fur. The fur is dark brown or black.

A star-nosed mole has a long, rounded body. It has short legs. Its front feet are wide with large claws. It has a long tail covered in fur.

Star-nosed moles are small. Adults are five to eight inches (13 to 20 cm) long. They weigh less than three ounces (85 g).

Did You Know?

A star-nosed mole's feet have pink skin and dark scales.

BODY

CLAW

TENTACLE

LEG

FOOT

TAIL

What a Star!

The star-nosed mole is named for its unusual nose. Each **nostril** is surrounded by 11 pink, fleshy **tentacles**. The tentacles spread out in the shape of a star.

The **sensitive** star is always moving. It is only about the size of a human fingertip. But, it is five times more sensitive to touch than an entire human hand!

A star-nosed mole's tentacles may give it the best sense of touch of any mammal!

Unusual but Useful

A star-nosed mole's strange-looking tentacles are very useful. The mole uses them to feel its surroundings and find prey. The tentacles can also cover its nostrils. This keeps dirt out of its nose when the mole is digging.

Did You Know?

Star-nosed moles have good senses of hearing and smell.

Because they tunnel underground, star-nosed moles don't rely on their sense of sight. In fact, scientists believe they are mostly blind.

Where in the World?

Star-nosed moles are found in North America. They live in the eastern United States and southeastern Canada.

Star-nosed moles live in many **habitats**. They prefer areas with wet soil. This includes forests, meadows, and marshes. Star-nosed moles are often found near streams, lakes, and ponds.

North
America

Europe

= Star-Nosed
Mole Region

Africa

Atlantic Ocean

Pacific Ocean

South
America

N
W   E
S

Digging Machines

Star-nosed moles are skilled at digging tunnels. Their wide front feet scoop large amounts of dirt. And, their strong claws break through hard-packed dirt.

A star-nosed mole can dig seven to eight feet (2 to 3 m) of tunnel in one hour.

15

Star-nosed moles dig tunnels that are about one to two and a half inches (3 to 6 cm) wide. Some tunnels are just below ground. Others are two feet (0.6 m) deep.

A star-nosed mole's tunnel often includes a nest. Nests are built in dry areas. For safety, they are often located where the tunnel passes under stumps or logs. They may be lined with dry leaves or grass.

Sometimes, star-nosed moles search for food above ground. This is unusual for a mole.

17

Water Lovers

Most moles do not like water. But, star-nosed moles are good swimmers and divers.

A star-nosed mole's wide front feet act like paddles. Its tentacles plug its nose. The mole can stay underwater for about ten seconds.

Did You Know?

Star-nosed moles even swim under ice during winter!

Some star-nosed mole tunnels open right at or just below the water's surface.

A Mole's Life

Often, many star-nosed moles live in the same area. Some scientists believe they form loose groups called colonies. Colonies often include moles from the same family.

Star-nosed moles are active all year, even during cold winters. These animals are active during the day and at night. They spend about half of each day resting.

Did You Know?
Scientists aren't sure whether the moles in a colony share tunnels.

Sometimes, star-nosed moles run over or dig through snow to find food.

21

Star-nosed moles are in greater danger of being hunted than other moles. That is because they spend more time out of their tunnels.

When not in their tunnels, star-nosed moles have many **predators**. On the ground, owls, hawks, foxes, skunks, and weasels hunt them. Under water, minks and large fish hunt them.

Star-nosed moles are the only mole to live in wetlands. So in addition to predators, habitat loss is also a danger.

Favorite Foods

Star-nosed moles hunt prey underground. This includes earthworms and young beetles. They also seek food underwater. This includes leeches, mollusks, fish, and young insects.

Did You Know?

A star-nosed mole's tail grows thicker during winter. The mole stores fat there to use as energy.

Star-nosed moles are known for hunting and eating their prey quickly.

Life Cycle

A female star-nosed mole gives birth to three to seven babies. A newborn mole is tiny and its skin is bare. Its eyes and ears are closed. The **tentacles** on its nose are folded flat. It drinks its mother's milk and grows.

After about two weeks, a young mole's eyes, ears, and star begin to work. At about three to four weeks old, a star-nosed mole is ready to live on its own.

A newborn star-nosed mole
has wrinkly, light pink skin.

World Wide Weird

Star-nosed moles are common in their territory. Although these animals are not in danger now, it is important to know how our actions affect wild animals. With care, we can keep weird, wonderful animals such as star-nosed moles around for years to come.

Scientists aren't sure how long star-nosed moles live in the wild. They believe it may be three to four years.

FAST FACTS ABOUT:
Star-Nosed Moles

Animal Type – mammal

Size – 5 to 8 inches (13 to 20 cm) long

Weight – less than 3 ounces (85 g)

Habitat – forests, meadows, and marshes with wet soil in eastern United States and southeastern Canada

Diet – earthworms, leeches, mollusks, fish, and young insects

What makes the star-nosed mole wildly weird?

It has 22 super-sensitive tentacles on its nose and it is a strong swimmer, even during the winter!

Glossary

habitat a place where a living thing is naturally found.

mammal a member of a group of living beings. Mammals make milk to feed their babies and usually have hair or fur on their skin.

nostril an opening of a nose.

predator a person or animal that hunts and kills animals for food.

prey an animal hunted or killed by a predator for food.

sensitive able to quickly and easily feel or notice.

tentacle a long, slender body part that often grows around the mouth or the head of some animals.

Websites

To learn more about World's Weirdest Animals, visit **booklinks.abdopublishing.com**. These links are routinely monitored and updated to provide the most current information available.

Index